# A Tea Bag

*F. Post Casto*

WestBow
PRESS
A DIVISION OF THOMAS NELSON

ISBN: 978-1-4497-5625-3 (sc)
ISBN: 978-1-4497-5626-0 (e)

Library of Congress Control Number: 2012910734

WestBow Press books may be ordered through booksellers or by contacting:

WestBow Press
A Division of Thomas Nelson
1663 Liberty Drive
Bloomington, IN 47403
www.westbowpress.com
1-(866) 928-1240

Printed in the United States of America

WestBow Press rev. date: 06/15/12

# Contents

# Foreword

Who the Author of this book is, is wholly unnecessary to the Public, as the Object for Attention is the Doctrine itself, not the Man writing it. Yet, it may be necessary to say, that the man is unconnected with any political party, and under no sort of influence, public or private, but the influence of reason, principle, equality, individual freedom, and a belief in GOD.

The original intent of this book was to define and correct deficiencies in the Constitution with rationalization as to why the change is necessary. After several versions and rewrites it became apparent that the evil of socialism that has crept into our system of laws and justice must also be addressed. Then it became apparent that to explain socialism, I must also address my belief in GOD.

If you, the reader, are hard core socialist, then stop reading here. This book does not expand upon the idea that the Government is the God. Government is good only when it follows the divine (or cosmic) laws of GOD. When man decides that he is smarter than GOD and deviates from the divine law, then corruption of the Government ensues.

Our Founding Fathers understood most of the concepts of divine law and wrote the Constitution accordingly. It took a very bloody revolution, ninety years later (the civil war), to remove portions of the Constitution that went against divine law. But citizens were motivated to do right in the eyes of GOD. This book does not advocate another bloody revolution. It does concede that citizens have the right to stand up and be counted for GOD and Country.

# Chapter 1
## *A Dream*

In 2002 I had a dream. In that dream I was standing before the throne of GOD. A voice said, "You will go and judge America."

I replied, "I can not. I don't know how or what to judge."

"Well spoken. It is good that you know your limits. Then you will be a lightening rod and they will judge themselves."

"I don't understand."

"You have been given a sword of truth and a shield of honesty; go."

I awoke thinking, "What kind of strange dream was that?" Then I promptly forgot about it as being just another weird dream that has no meaning. I never connected the dream to my life's events.

My position was terminated in 2004 and I was forced to find another job. Thinking that I had no chance, I applied for a Government job in Iraq. Again, to my amazement, I was in Iraq within a month. Fourteen months later I was terminated because a person did not like how I blew the dust and dirt out of my nose. That was the reason given for my termination.

I tried to get my job back. The Government had violated OPM and DOD regulations, an Executive Order, and EEOC laws, but I was not reinstated. For years I fought through Agency boards, Administrative Courts, and Federal District Court. Every judge found some little loophole to deny my claim. I became despondent. I had one last little hope, the Federal Appeals Court. In 2008, I began the process of the appeal.

Then, I had another dream. In that dream, I was standing before the throne of GOD. A voice said, "Your ordeal is ended. If they had acted with integrity and justice, I would have given them cheap, abundant energy and prosperity. But they have judged themselves as lacking. They will see these things: gasoline will cost $4.00 a gallon, trillions of dollars will be removed from the economy, and the zero-year curse will be ended. I will give them exactly what they ask for: a task master who will beat them into the ground. And none shall stop him, for I have ordained it."

It wasn't until the second dream that I remembered the first dream, and it became clear. I half heartedly filed the Federal Appeals Court paperwork. I knew in my heart that America had lost this battle against darkness.

I often wondered about these dreams. Why would GOD punish the people and not limit the punishment to the Government? Looking at the prophecy HE had given; the first two were very generic. But the third was rather strange and on the surface sounded good. How could it be bad to lift a curse?

I researched the "zero-year curse." No president elected in a zero year has been able to complete his term in office. Either his body or his mind suffered an untimely death. The curse is attributed to a Native American Christian medicine man. His tribe had a treaty with the government, and in a land grab, the treaty was broken by the Government.

## Zero-Year Presidential Curse

| Elected | President | Cause |
|---|---|---|
| 1840 | William H. Harrison | Pneumonia |
| 1860 | Abraham Lincoln | Assassinated |
| 1880 | James A. Garfield | Assassinated |
| 1900 | William McKinley | Assassinated |
| 1920 | Warren G. Harding | Heart attack |
| 1940 | Franklin D. Roosevelt | Cerebral hemorrhage |
| 1960 | John F. Kennedy | Assassinated |
| 1980 | Ronald Reagan | Alzheimer's |

But surely not having the president die or be incapacitated was a blessing and not a curse. In 2008, George W. Bush became the first president since 1840 to complete his zero-year-elected term in office. The curse was broken.

The prophecy I was given was just that: prophecy, things to come. But there had to be a deeper meaning. The zero-year curse was a curse upon the Government. What would be accomplished if that curse were lifted? It took a long time to sink into my brain. The government was being removed as the responsible party. The people were to be held accountable. Why would HE hold the people accountable? The Government is "of the people, by the people, for the people." It all fell into place. The people had allowed the Government to run wild. The people were to be held accountable for the Government's actions. The people did not exercise control over the government and pull in the reins.

Twice GOD gave a warning to the people but the people did not heed HIS warnings. On 12 September 2001, Tom Daschle, in a joint meeting of both houses, laid a curse on the United States. On 11 September 2004, John Edwards issued the same curse. The curse was finalized in 2008, when Barack Obama issued the same curse. The curse came straight from the Bible. Isaiah 9:10; "The bricks are fallen down, but we will build with hewn stone: the sycamores are cut down, but we will replant cedars."

This Verse tickled the politicians' fancy. It sounded good to the ears. Three times, by three different political leaders, this verse was quoted in reply to the events of 9/11. The people loved the words. There was no hue or outcry because of these words. Either no one who heard the words had read the Bible or they did not realize that it was a curse and not a blessing.

Verse 10 is not a standalone verse. It must be read in conjunction with the verses before and after. Let me paraphrase what it says, "I, the LORD, chastise the people… who say in pride and stoutness of heart. The bricks are fallen down, but we will build with hewn stone: the sycamores are cut down, but we will replant cedars. Therefore, the LORD shall set Satan against them and shall join their enemies together to devour them. For the people turneth not unto the LORD…For the leaders of this people cause them to err."

This clearly states that America will feel the wrath of GOD, because we did not accept GOD's chastisement on 9/11. We will rebuild the towers. We will punish those who hurt us. The few ministers that understood and tried to warn the people were ignored. We will not look to GOD for leadership. We will not look for honesty and truth in a leader. HE gave us exactly what we wanted a slick talking Chicago lawyer.

# Chapter 2
## *Socialism*

Socialism is an idealistic political system based upon 100 percent of the people producing 100 percent of the time. In Russia at the time of its collapse, it was estimated that 30 percent of the people were producing 50 percent of the time. The system could not support itself and it collapsed.

Since just before World War I, America has had a long list of leaders that define themselves as progressive, communist, socialist, or liberal. A rose by any other name is still a rose. The title they used doesn't matter. They were smarter than us common people. They knew how to run the people's lives to get the maximum return on their investment. It started out very slowly. Progressive income tax was the first big push. Why should poor people pay taxes? The rich people have the money; let them pay the taxes. To the working person, the philosophy sounded simple. But there was a hidden agenda. If the majority of people didn't pay taxes, then they wouldn't care how the money was spent. The Government then developed a philosophy that for every problem there was a solution: throw money at it. If the problem went away, then they could claim credit for resolving it. If the problem didn't go away, that was even better. They could raise taxes and drive more people into poverty. Remember the hidden agenda: people in poverty are too busy trying to live and are less likely to take an interest in what the Government is actually doing.

The problem grew with a long list of entitlement programs, e.g., social security insurance, unemployment insurance, etc. This forced even more people to depend upon the Government. It was self-perpetuating. It was socialistic dreams come true, that is, until World War II. The National Socialist German Workers (Nazi) Party was determined to rule the world. The socialist powers in America didn't want to share their power with another socialist group. They relaxed their socialist push in order to fight the Nazi party. World War II gave us, the people, a little reprieve from their relentless push.

You would think that watching Russia fall would tell the socialists that socialism is a farce and doesn't work. It's just the opposite; they are more determined than ever to destroy our freedom.

As a college student, I was often approached by Young Communist Party members trying to recruit me. One of their main arguments was, "Wouldn't you love to live in a country where everyone was truly equal?" I would let them talk for hours and even encourage them from time to time, with an enthusiastic "YES! YES!" When they reached the climax of their speech and were about to broach the question of my joining, I would calmly say, "Yes, it would be great; no more government to rule over me."

They then had to explain that government is necessary, "But you have to have a government to built necessary infrastructure, such as roads and bridges to transport goods and hospitals and fire departments to take care of people, and, that this ideal socialistic government is so much better for the collective good of the people than the American form of government."

Whereupon I would immediately use the same arguments they used against me and my Government. I would direct it back at them. "But, if you have a government, then you have leaders. If you have leaders, then you don't have total equality, because the leaders will always want and get special treatment." Then they would try to explain that leaders deserved special privileges, because they did so much more work leading us. And I would counter that it was not total equality. The argument would start in earnest.

After a while they would realize that I couldn't be converted to their way of viewing life. They would give up and move away from the weirdo who wanted to live in a world without government or specially privileged leaders. They probably did believe it was a beautiful government. And they probably believed they would be the ones on top, with everyone working for them. Stop and think about it. No more individual thinking. The government would direct every action and fulfill every desire, wish, and whim. It is time to pop your bubble. The only place socialism really works is in the movies. That is why so many movie stars are socialists; it is all make believe. In reality, it is only some petty tyrant wanting you to march to the beat of his drum. Socialism is nothing but a form of slavery. The only difference is that progressive socialism allows you to willingly become slaves by feeding you beautiful lies.

The other main argument the Young Communists used was just as insidious, "Couldn't you use an extra thirty thousand dollars?" Who wouldn't say YES to that? I would let them talk about taking all the money away from the rich and dividing it among the poor such that everyone would get an equal share of all the money. They would spout off large numbers. And your share will be thirty thousand dollars.

Again I would wait until their climax and then, "But if everyone has it, it is not worth anything." It was like hitting them between the eyes with a sledge hammer. I actually had one say to me, "But you're not supposed to think that way."

Then I would drive the nail home, "If everyone has thirty thousand dollars and I want to buy a car that originally cost thirty thousand, the dealer will raise the price to sixty thousand. That first thirty thousand is equal to zero." The price of everything will shoot through the roof, mainly because everyone has money and no one will be producing. If you can't keep your profits; why would you produce? Again they would walk away shaking their heads, wondering why a person would want to protect those rich mongers of capitalism and not give it to those that don't want to work.

Our Founding Fathers made several mistakes. That is one of those statements that no one likes to see in print. The biggest mistake was that they looked only at the good side of mankind and wrote the Constitution accordingly. Just like socialism, it only works in the movies, not in real life. They could not envision people wanting power just because it was there for the taking. Greed can take many forms; not always money. Some people want power over other people just to show the world how important they are. It is the power they want. The money is just an added bonus.

Remember this chapter as you read the proposed Amendments. Look for the insidious hand of socialism that is working to take away our freedom.

# Chapter 3
## *Legalizing Amendments*

Our leaders learned a lot from the rulers of Nazi Germany. The biggest thing they learned was that if you tell a lie to the people long enough; soon they will believe it to be the truth. Nowhere in the Constitution does it say that Church and State must be separated. It has been beat into our head so deeply that we believe it is there. Even the Supreme Court believes it is in the Constitution. I dare anyone out there to read the Constitution and find it. It doesn't exist.

Most people, including Barack Obama, believe that any law passed by Congress is part of the Constitution. This is also a fable. An Amendment may not be passed without 75 percent of states' approval. Even the people that know Congress may submit an Amendment to the Constitution think that the people must approve the Amendment. This is also wrong. The Constitution requires 75 percent of the states to approve an Amendment before it can become part of the Constitution.

The Constitution was not written by a bunch of ignorant farmers. It was written by some of the most intelligent people on this planet. The Founding Fathers setup a government system unlike any seen before. There was no "Writing a Constitution for Dummies." From scratch, they came up with the idea of freedom: something the world had never seen before. Then they tried to put the idea of freedom into a usable form of government with checks and balances to make it self correcting.

Three branches of government were identified; Legislative, Judicial, and Executive.

The Legislative branch was to generate and pass laws and was broken into two subparts, the Senate and the House. The Senate was to represent the interests of State governments and to provide controls over the Executive branch. The House was to represent the interest of the citizens and provide control over the budget.

The Executive branch was to enforce the written laws and control the military. Signature of the President on a legislative bill was to confirm that the Executive branch could enforce a particular law. A veto was the President telling Congress that it could not enforce the bill as written.

The Judicial branch was to rule upon the Constitutionality of the law, impose justice through the authority of a jury of peers, and impose sentence as defined in the written laws.

Down through the years various people have redefined their roles under the Constitution to suit their personal desires for power over, WE, the people. Through this abuse the Constitution has slowly eroded and lost its meaning as the cornerstone that all other laws are based upon.

Added to this is the fact that the Founding Fathers made basic assumptions about the future and these assumptions did not materialize. An examples best illustrates this: They assumed all immigrants would come from Europe and be Judo-Christian oriented. They did not visualize people from all over the world coming to America. Freedom of religion was meant to be freedom without dictate from the Governments as to the sect of worship of Jesus Christ.

The Founding Fathers, knew that evil would creep in. They realized, even as they wrote the Constitution, that it was not perfect and would contain errors or be purposely misinterpreted by self seeking individuals. Therefore, they advanced a Constitutional Amendment process to correct these kinds of problems.

Three quarters of the State Legislatures must ratify an Amendment to the Constitution for the Amendment to become Law. This is the clearly defined mandate in the Constitution. As a sideline, it also states that Congress may initiate the Amendment process. However, it did not exclude other methods of proposing or submitting an Amendment. Therefore, three quarters of the State Legislatures must ratify these Amendments for these Amendments to become Law. Congress will moan and groan if these Amendments becomes law, but they had their chance to save America and they blew it.

Subsequent Chapters in this book shall be the Amendments, in italics, and the summarized logic behind each Amendment will follow. There will be Amendments that you, the reader, will dislike and do not think we need. There will be Amendments that you, the reader, will like, and want instituted. The object of these Amendments is to rein in big government and make it more responsive to, WE, the People. It cannot be geared for any one person or any one group of people. By its nature it must be geared for all of the people, all of the time. These Amendments should be taken as a whole.

Stop here for a word of caution to the reader. America is a country of self reliant individuals. There are some people, even citizens of this country, that believe the government can do a better job of managing and controlling their lives. These people will try to distract you. They will point out one or two items and tell you that the whole thing is a bad idea. These Amendments were written as a whole, all of the points are interconnected. Like a brick building, leave one brick out and the whole structure is weakened.

Do not make a snap decision, read the entire book. Do not believe anyone if they try to tell you what is in this book. Read the book for yourself. Then, and only then, can YOU make a rational, informed decision. Only then can you argue for it or against it. If you, the reader, find that you are in agreement with most of the Amendments then tell your friends. If you, the reader, find that you oppose most of these Amendments, then you are probably a socialist and you should migrate to another country that is more in tune with your ideals, maybe China. America really doesn't need you.

Below are the Amendments in entirety. Each Amendment, in italics, was written as narrow as possible, but, not so narrow as to stifle the intent. Conversely, it can not be so broad as to allow an intrusive government. It has been very difficult to find a middle ground.

We have been too long in our complacency, allowing other people to do our thinking for us. Yes, these Amendments have major changes that will affect every person in this country. Sometimes the cure is worse than the disease itself. It is an old saying that fits this situation. Our country has a disease, it is fast dying. We have learned to live with this cancer that is slowly eating away our freedoms. Curing this disease will involve upheaval and change. It is a big pill to take and it will be hard to swallow. But it will prolong the life of our country. It is your choice, support it and America, or oppose it watch our country die. Whatever you decide, I will support your choice. I am an American and that is the American way. As an American, I might not like your decision but I will support your right to make that decision.

*WE, the Citizens propose the following Amendments to the Constitution of the United States, with the desire that they be submitted to the full fifty State Legislatures, to correct deficiencies identified within our present system of government. The following will immediately become law upon ratification by thirty eight states, unless otherwise identified in the individual Amendment.*

# Chapter 4
## *Amendment XXVIII*

*Jurisprudence is hereby abolished as the Law of the Land. All Courts of Law are hereby restricted from creating governing Laws. The function of the Supreme Court shall be limited in scope to declaring Laws and judicial decisions of lower courts as being in accordance with the Constitution.*

Ask almost any Federal District or Appeals Court judge how they think the Constitution fits into the laws of this country. The majority will say the Constitution is mote. It is not worth the paper it is written upon. Then ask why. They will tell you that jurisprudence has replaced the Constitution and that jurisprudence is the all encompassing law of the land. The Constitution is too narrowly defined to be of much use

Jurisprudence is the concept that a Judge's decision is sanctimonious and therefore is the law to be applied to all similar cases. Attorneys spend years learning and regurgitating Judge's decisions, not the law. Judge's decisions carry more weight then the laws that were duly authorized by representatives of the people. This practice of having laws that only attorneys know exist goes against the very principles set up by the Founding Fathers. The function of the judge is to interpret the law, as written, against the unique circumstances of each case. It was never envisioned that a Judge would ignore the written law and hear arguments about which prior Judge's decision is applicable to a particular case. This has become a ploy of attorneys to prolong court battles to make money. Don't get me wrong, I am not against finding ways for people to make money. But cheating people by subverted justice is not an acceptable practice. Let the lawyers argue the laws, as written. Each case must be tried on its own merits against the written law.

# Chapter 5
## *Amendment XXIX*

*Courts shall heretofore hold individuals responsible for their actions. Common sense and the prevailing set of shared attitudes, values, goals, and practices that characterizes the American people, to include traditions, ideals, customs, beliefs, and values; e.g., democracy, capitalism, monotheism, civil liberties; shall take legal precedent over any contrary external culture.*

In civil and criminal cases rational common sense must take precedence. People must take responsibility for their actions. A free person should never debase themselves to say someone or some events made them do it. Even the socialist countries do not allow such a senseless defense. Yet, American Courts willingly allow it.

Everyone has heard about the woman that bought a hot cup of coffee and held it between her legs while driving. Common sense would dictate that the movement of the legs to effect driving would create a problem. Yet, the courts ruled that the maker of the coffee made it too hot and that caused her to be scalded. Common sense was not allowed as a defense. She burned herself because someone else made it too hot; not because she put it in a dangerous position; not because she had to slam on the brakes to avoid an accident.

The court ruled that she had no responsibility to put it in a safe place.

American values should never be subjugated to a foreign belief or value that in any way harms American values. Example: We do not stone to death a woman that goes to the mall without a male relative. This is anathema to American morals, values, and beliefs. Yet, we are being pushed to allow foreign culture to dictate how our laws are being applied. At this time it is only a gentle push to honor foreign Holidays. But, just like entitlement programs, it will grow beyond that gentle push. You will regret it when Cinco de Mayo becomes a Federal Holiday.

# Chapter 6
## *Amendment XXX*

*Legal tender and property, with an aggregate value over one thousand dollars, may not be confiscated without due process of law by a jury of peers. Legal tender and property, with an aggregate value less than one thousand dollars is exempt from confiscation.*

In recent years laws have been passed allowing the Government to confiscate properties for nefarious reasons. A police officer pulls a person over for speeding and asks to search the vehicle. In the search they find $500 dollars in a wallet in the glove compartment. It is obviously drug money and is summarily confiscated without due process. The citizen has no recourse and cannot recover the monies. In this example the police officer has been delegated the roles of judge, jury, and executioner. The Declaration of Independence list jury trial and due process over thirty times and was the main reason for the American Revolution. Confiscation should only be by order of a jury of peers.

# Chapter 7
## *Amendment XXXI*

*Eminent Domain is hereby abolished. A legal entity cannot be deprived of their legally owned property for public uses without their express consent.*

Eminent Domain started out as an English law. The King could commandeer any property for the good of the nation. It was and is an English law. It has no basis in American law, except that the Supreme Court ruled that the Government could do it. The American Government saw it as a good thing. Forts had to be built in key locations to protect the citizens.

Then it expanded; roads, courthouses, and post offices had to be built. This began the descent of Eminent Domain. The Government always wanted the choice property to build their facilities. Beginning in the 1930s, governments at all levels began abusing the right of Eminent Domain. A prime example was the Skyline Drive project in Virginia. Thousands of acres were confiscated to create a park with a long winding road. The great public need for the land and road was to give the politicians in Washington a place to take a long leisurely drive through the country to look at the color change of the autumn leaves.

Now it has gone to the point that a government may confiscate your property and give or sell it to another private individual. The argument is made that the second individual is going to make the property more valuable and increase the tax base for the Government. Something is horribly wrong with this picture. The Government can arbitrary take your property and give it to another person. Where does this process stop? Let's take this to the extreme. Someday the Government could take your children and give them to another person, because the other person is not collecting welfare for your child.

The tax base is more important to the Government than citizen's rights. Citizen rights will not exist if the government wants what a Citizen has and is allowed to summarily take it. The right of an individual to own property should be sacrosanct.

When the Government abuses its power, then that power should be taken away. The rights of the citizen are more important than the rights of the Government.

# Chapter 8
## *Amendment XXXII*

*Courts and legal boards shall not subjugate a jury decision without due process of law by a jury of peers.*

Courts routinely review jury decisions and change the outcome to suit their whim. Case in point: Recently the Snyder family sued a church for obstructing their son's funeral. The suit was based upon pain and suffering. The jury found the church guilty of causing needless pain and suffering. However, the appeals court said the jury was in error and reversed the decision. Now the Snyder family must pay the church. The court ruled that the original jury wasn't intelligent enough to make a rational decision. I'm surprised the Judge didn't find the jury in contempt and give them jail time. Why even bother to have a jury trial if some Judge can change the outcome on a whim.

The American Revolution started because British judges would summarily pass judgment without jury input. It is mentioned thirty seven (37) times in the Declaration of Independence. Perhaps our founding fathers thought it was important to have a jury of peers pass judgment. Now we have jury input but judges and boards still ignore it. We need to put the courts back into the hands of the people.

The other case in point is the legal boards, e.g., parole boards. The jury finds a defendant guilty of three heinous murders and sentence is passed for three life terms in prison. The parole board is told they need to free up bed space for more inmates. They release the guy after ten years. He goes out and murders more people. This was not the original intent of the sentencing. This board has subverted the trial by jury process. Their subversion of the process was not based upon evidence of the crime committed. It was not approved by a jury of peers.

Why even bother having a jury of peers? The Judge and the boards know what is best for us. In true socialist thinking, let the Government take care of it. The common people are too ignorant to know what is right.

# Chapter 9
## *Amendment XXXIII*

*Use or brandishment of a deadly weapon, e.g., firearm or edged weapon, during a convicted felonious act shall carry a minimum term of incarceration for life. A second time conviction of child molestation or of forced rape or of human trafficking or any combination thereof shall carry a minimum term of incarceration for life.*

Most people would say that this Amendment does not belong in the Constitution, that this is common law. I agree, but, common law is at the whim of corrupt local politicians and unscrupulous judges. The purpose of having a Federal government is to codify areas not consistently enforced by all states. This standardizes the penalty across all states and the most heinous criminals are permanently removed from society to protect live and limb of citizens.

Owning and using a weapon is a citizen right. Violating that right by using it in the commission of a felonious act should be a federal crime.

Life, liberty, and pursuit of happiness is also a citizen right. Violating that right in the commission of a felonious act should be a federal crime.

# Chapter 10
## *Amendment XXXIV*

*The separation of the Judicial Branch from the Legislative Branch shall be meticulously maintained. To this end, the Legislative Branch shall contain no elected official who has been or is authorized to practice law. Present office holders are excluded until their next scheduled election.*

A long habit of not thinking a thing is wrong, gives it a superficial appearance of it being right. Attorneys now are the dominant group in Congress. Most people assume that this is correct. Who better to write laws than attorneys? This is the wrong answer. It means attorneys now control all three branches of the government. This is a conflict of interest. Lawyers are making laws that they use to judge, prosecute, and defend citizens. To make all citizens equal in the eyes of the law, the requirement to hold a law degree to become a judge, prosecutor, or lawyer should be discontinued. Since this is impractical; the lawyers' guild would never allow such a thing; the only way to remove this injustice is to bar lawyers from creating the laws.

# Chapter 11
## *Amendment XXXV*

*Members of Congress shall be limited to two full terms, collectively, in their office. Present office holders are excluded until their next scheduled election.*

The founding fathers envisioned rotating elected officials. After a stint in office a person was expected to return to their given profession; doctor, engineer, bartender, or wheel maker. A career politician was then and is now an oxymoron. This is a major point that our Founding Fathers missed, power corrupts. Once in office and tasting the forbidden fruit of power, office holders do not want to leave.

George Washington saw this as a personal constriction and stepped down after two terms. He recognized the corrupting influence of power. Even the power of the Senate or House can corrupt. Office holders must be churned to eliminate (reduce) the scum on top of the pond. No one person should be allowed to hold an office, House or Senate or combination thereof for more than two full terms. Notice that this does not restrict Congressmen and Senators from running for President.

# Chapter 12
## *Amendment XXXVI*

*Public monies shall not be used to fund travel by members of Congress outside the borders of the United States to foreign countries.*

House and Senate members are constantly running around the globe at taxpayer expense. They have no legitimate reason to travel to a foreign country to conduct American business. It clearly states in the Constitution that this is a function of the Executive Branch. The job of the Legislative Branch is to run the United States, not other countries. Therefore, tax monies should not be used to finance their traveling. If they or their wives or mistresses want to take a vacation in a foreign country, let them pay for it.

Since some states, e.g., Alaska, are not contiguous, a slight disclaimer, *to foreign countries*, was made to allow travel to those states, as long as they do not schedule a lay over in a foreign country..

Readers: In the example above, I used e.g. (for instance) in place of i.e. (in essence) because at some future time more states may be added that are not contiguous. These Amendments are to fix problems now. But, the ultimate goal is to provide a better Constitution for your children and future generations.

# Chapter 13
## *Amendment XXXVII*

*All laws shall apply equally to all citizens including elected and appointed officials and Government agencies.*

Working most of my adult life around Washington, I have heard, on numerous occasions, "Our agency is exempt from that law." Plus Congress is constantly adds little perks to their job, such as free lunch.

I know of a lawsuit against the Government that was thrown out of court because the laws didn't apply to the Government. Age discrimination does not apply to the Government. Equal Employment Opportunity does not apply to the Government. Executive Orders are only guidelines that cannot be enforced by the courts.

Funny, I thought all laws applied equally to all legal entities. Looks like we need it in the Constitution to make it so and take some of these unwritten rules away from the Government. In this hodge-podge of laws, how am I, just an ordinary citizen, supposed to know which laws apply and which do not?

NOTE: The continuous lawsuit may be viewed:

United States Merit System Protection Board; Docket DC-3443-06-0245-I-1

United States District Court for Eastern Virginia; Docket 1:06cv00933

United States District Court for Eastern Virginia; Docket 1:06cv01147

United States Court of Appeals for Fourth District; Docket 08-1143

# Chapter 14
## *Amendment XXXVIII*

*Any legislation submitted for consideration shall be limited to one subject. The final version shall be in common use English and is limited to a maximum of ten normal size pages, containing normal size print. The final version shall be made available for a seven day review by the public before consideration for passage. Excluded from the time limit of this article is a Declaration of War. Excluded from the page limit of this article is the Budget.*

This is to eliminate the late Sunday night passage of legislation that no one has had time to read. Changes to the final version, even while being debated for passage, creates a new version that would require a new waiting period.

The waiting period will allow for a cooling off period for emotionally charged legislation. The Founding Fathers repeatedly cautioned against emotionally charged legislation, preferring dispassionate, rational decisions. A fearful herd of sheep are easily driven over the edge of a precipice. Most politicians know this and use emotion to force legislation for their secret agenda.

Limiting subject and number of pages shall reduce confusion. Present day politicians need the confusion of 2000 page documents covering several subjects to hide their secret agenda from the public. This will bring everything into the open for an honest review. A hidden or secret agenda would become obvious to the public.

Notice that the Budget is not exempt from the time limit of this clause. Citizens and watchdog groups will now have time to review the budget and register complaints and warnings.

I had to make this Amendment longer than I wanted. Every detail had to be clearly defined. I didn't want to give Congress the excuse to use sheets of paper as big as a greyhound bus. Plus I don't want them to use number 2 font. So small it would take a magnifying glass to be able to read it.

Congress: Please use the KISS principle in creating documents; Keep It Simple Stupid.

# Chapter 15
## *Amendment XXXIX*

*A citizen shall not be required to reimburse the government for incarceration, judicial proceeding, or other normal judicial services provided to citizens.*

A five dollar fine suddenly becomes three hundred dollars after court costs, prison/jail fees, recording costs, and a host of other fees and costs is added to the fine. This is a ploy of the courts to tax citizens without regard to equality or getting the legislative branches involved. Some people will say that the legislative branch was involved by passing a law allowing these fees. But that logic misconstrues the intent. The intent is to take the power of budget control away from the legislative branch. The courts now have their private budget that is in no way controlled by the legislative branch.

Monies to run the court system shall only come from the budget.

This is my personal complaint. So many things require a service fee. It costs $75.00 for a passport. But a passport is one of the required documents to prove citizenship to get a job. In essence, they charge me $75.00 dollars to get a job but still hire millions of illegal aliens.

# Chapter 16
## *Amendment XL*

*The printing of monies shall not be based upon debt, with exception for periods of declared war and up to three years after hostilities have cease; a declining annual GDP; or in the event of a major natural disaster and one year after the disaster. Printed money shall be based upon noble metals. The Federal Reserve shall no longer be allowed to print money based upon debt.*

In the 1930s America went off the gold standard. Up until that time a dollar was worth a dollar. The 1930 prevailing economic philosophy was to borrow money, let the money inflate, then, pay back the loan with the inflated money. This may be hard to understand. Inflated money is valued less than real money. Inflated money is a hidden tax. As the value of money goes down; prices go up. The four dollar gasoline you buy now was twenty five cents in the 1950s. Where does the extra three dollars and seventy five cents go? It is a hidden tax.

Money should be based upon some valuable asset, i.e., noble metals (gold, silver, etc.).
Money would then be stable and never go up or down in value.

At present the Federal Reserve prints money based upon the debt they hold. If they receive a bank note that a million dollars has been borrowed then they print another million dollars and lend it to the banks. It is a vicious cycle. They control the rate of lending by the interest rate. Since the interest rate is not based on supply and demand, there are no checks and balances. The only check is the interest rate they decide to charge. It is a house made with playing cards. The first gust of wind knocks it down. That is exactly what happened with the housing market. Too many people defaulted on their debt. The money printed based upon their debt now became worthless.

This practice of inflated money to make us look rich must be stopped. It is a hidden tax that our Government is responsible for; that means you and I must pay it. I want my money based upon something solid and tangible. The Secretary of the Treasury should be held accountable for the printing of all money.

The Federal Reserve Board is a quasi Government agency. It controls printing of money and fixing the interest rate. It operates outside of Government control. This board must be dissolved. Article 1; Section 8 of the Constitution clearly states, Congress shall coin money. Congress did not want to do its job. They gave it to an uncontrolled agency. Put it back the way the Founding Fathers envisioned.

# Chapter 17
## *Amendment XLI*

*Departments, Agencies, or Commissions shall not be delegated congressional authority without Congress maintaining oversight.*

In the 1940's, the Screw Commission was established to control measurements of nuts, bolts, and screws for the war effort. To my knowledge, this Commission has not met in over forty years. If they have, then the meetings are secret, because no minutes could be found in the public records. However, it has a payroll and spends our money. This is what happens when there is no oversight. Wish I had a job like that, draw a big paycheck and not do any work. Mr. Congressman, I want to apply for this job

Repeatedly Congress gives Congressional authority to Agencies, Departments, and Commissions. But they frequently forget, intentional or absentminded, to put restrictions and oversight controls. But then it gets worse. The group given the responsibility then parcels out that responsibility.

Case in Point: Let's look at the Equal Employment Opportunity Commission. They were given authority to control equal employment. Their first order of business was to make all Departments responsible for the initial claim and response. What happens when a claim is filed but the responsible Department doesn't respond to the claim? If you contact EEOC they will tell you they can't do anything because the responsible Department did not respond. Take it to court and the judge will tell you that it is not his responsibility; it belongs to EEOC. And the circle continues.

This example came from an actual event with the Defense Intelligence Agency EEO.

# Chapter 18
## *Amendment XLII*

*Only Cabinet Heads appointed by the President and approved by the Senate shall wield power over their respective Department or Agency. Temporary appointments may be made to fill a vacancy, but only until the next meeting of Congress.*

"Approval by the Senate" is an original requirement of the Constitution. But Presidents found a loop hole. I can't find the right person to hold this position, so I am going to keep this temporary person in place forever.

We must return to the original intent of the Founding Fathers. A temporary person may be assigned until the next meeting of Congress. At that time the seat will again become vacant and it will remain vacant until permanently filled.

# Chapter 19
## *Amendment XLIII*

*Executive Orders shall not carry force of law.*

Executive orders were intended to convey orders concerning work habits within the Executive Branch. But agencies increasingly use them to impose changes outside of their respective agencies. Granted the boss should be able to give orders to employees. But, in the government sector, employees assume that a Presidential Order sets the law. This is to clarify that only Congress can pass laws, not the President. Presidential orders can only affect employees in the executive branch. Once an order affects any legal entity outside of the Executive Branch it becomes law. The President is not empowered to enact such laws. Therefore, such rules shall not enjoy the force of law. The President is only empowered to enforce the legally approved written laws.

# Chapter 20
## *Amendment XLIV*

*The military draft of individuals shall be re-instated through random drawing. There shall be no exemptions or exclusions from the draft of all militia able bodied citizens. Foreign nationals may volunteer to serve in the United States military and shall be rewarded with citizenship for themselves, spouse, and children after six years of faithful service. However, at no time may the number of foreign nationals exceed five percent of the military force.*

Having a professional military is the first step toward tyranny, by creating allegiance to the employer, i.e., the government; and not to the country as a whole. Therefore a professional military is not an acceptable practice. Conscripted personnel do not have this allegiance to the government and therefore provide a safety net against such tyranny. Too many citizens are afraid to serve their country and willingly allow the Government to do whatever it will. Conscription will broaden the education of the citizen base and will ultimately lead to a better, more informed decision making public.

Please notice, it says, "able bodied citizens." Women are not excluded from the draft. Women want to be equal. True equality is not just in benefits, it is also in responsibility.

There can be no greater responsibility than protecting our country.

Foreign personnel have allegiance to neither the government nor this country. Allegiance to America must be validated and, as a reward, citizenship allowed.

History, e.g., Rome, has shown that a high percentage mercenary army is a danger to the country hiring them. Therefore, we must restrict the number of mercenary personnel and foreign nationals in our military. If we can't defend ourselves, we should not expect to be free.

# Chapter 21
## *Amendment XLV*

*The President shall be limited to only appointing members of his immediate cabinet. The Political Appointee system at all levels of Government is hereby abolished.*

We have a Czar of this and a Czar of that. These Czars are supposedly advisors to the President. They have no official standing, except to draw a big paycheck. Numerous Political Appointees are in the same boat. Down through the years Presidents have said they need people loyal to them to keep tabs on all other employees. Homer Simpson says, "DOOH!"

Why do we have an Inspector General Department? Why do we have a Human Resources Departments? It is their job to keep tabs on employees. This political policy of giving our money away as political favors must stop.

I know, this will hurt the majority of you fun loving people out there. There will be no more Bill and Monica type jokes.

# Chapter 22
## *Amendment XLVI*

*The President shall not commence offensive military operations unless approved by Congress or a clearly defined threat of imminent attack is present.*

Starting with President Monroe, Presidents have staged offensive operations against other legitimate governments. More than once we have been warned to avoid foreign entanglements. This was another omission by our founding fathers in the Constitution. They did not envision that the American government would consider itself to be the peace keeper and protector of the world. Nor did they envision that Presidents would willy-nilly attack other countries.

Nowhere in the Constitution does it say that our Government is to spread our form of Government around the world. The job of the American government is to protect our citizens from enemies, foreign and domestic, but only on American soil. This protection does not extend to cover citizens that willingly leave American soil. Nor does it extend to protect citizens of other countries against the excesses of their Government.

The tree of liberty must be fertilized by blood. We have done a good job of fertilizing our liberty tree. Other countries must fertilize their tree if they want freedom.

# Chapter 23
## *Amendment XLVII*

*Amendment XVII to the Constitution of the United States is hereby rescinded in its entirety. Each State shall appoint, in such a manner as the legislature thereof may direct, two Senators. Present office holders are excluded until their next scheduled election. This is a State right that shall not be infringed.*

The Founding Fathers envisioned that a Senator would represent their respective state government and not the federal government. Most other countries have a National government. This means everything comes from their national government. A Federal Government means that the power is diluted to the State level. Our founding fathers envisioned a Federal Government that provided for common defense, dealing with foreign countries, the post office, and arbitrating disputes between the states.

The socialists realized that controlling 50 separate State Governments was too daunting a task. It was much easier to lie and control the mobs of people than to control 50 power hungry Governors. Congress decided that states should not be represented at the Federal level. Amendment XVII took away that control over the President. Since then, Presidents have expanded their power base. This has allowed the

Federal Government to have an almost unfettered approach to expanding into citizens lives.

This returns that power to the states, which was the original intent of the Constitution.

# Chapter 24
## *Amendment XLVIII*

*Amendment XXIII to the Constitution of the United States is hereby rescinded. Only legal States of the United States shall be represented in Congress. This is a State right that shall not be infringed.*

There is now a shadow Senator paid by the government to represent the District of Columbia. This Senator is allowed to attend committee meetings, introduce bills, and vote on issues. This concept holds the Founding Fathers in contempt and must be rescinded. The Founding Fathers visualized the District of Columbia as a neutral area, having no affiliation to any state or any state right issues that would divert the attention of Congress.

This Senator is a glorified lobbyist paid for by the government. As a Senator, he gets a government retirement package for doing such a great service for our country. I feel personally offended by this legitimized subversion of the Constitution.

Citizens living in the District of Columbia, that wish to be represented in Congress should move out of the neutral zone to a legitimate state.

# Chapter 25
## *Amendment XLIX*

*Within four years of passage of this Amendment, the United States Government shall remove itself from all control of the Educational System. The Educational System shall be a State right that shall not be infringed.*

The Constitution of the United States does not mention education. It was an assumed state right. Creation of the Department of Education was a power grab by the federal Government in violation of Tenth Amendment of the Constitution. This travesty must be corrected.

The biggest downfall of our educational system came when the federal government became involved. They didn't raise the standards as promised. For the common good, they lowered the standards so that no child was left behind. Can you imagine if they ran football the same way? Our hero, the halfback is a cripple that can't run. Every player has to walk slowly down the field to catch him. Well people that is what the government has done to our educational system.

Our educational system can't run down the field. It must walk slowly down the field so everyone can keep up. Life is so unfair. Not all of us get the beautiful woman as a wife. Not all of us get to be the big boss or own a fancy car.

Why should we handicap those that excel in academia? The Constitution guarantees us Life, Liberty, and the Pursuit of Happiness. No place in the Constitution does it say that we will achieve happiness or that all kids will come out of the public education system with the same level of knowledge.

This is socialistic thinking at its highest. What should we do with the kids that excel in learning, send them to the hospital and have half their brains removed?

# Chapter 26
## *Amendment L*

*No law, rule, or regulation shall be made or exist which gives special privileges, benefits, or burdens to any citizen or group or class of citizens, excluding prior treaties with the indigenous population. This is a citizen right that shall not be infringed.*

All hate crimes or anti-discrimination laws, rules, and regulations should be abolished. The present jumble of laws, rules, and regulations are, in and of themselves, discriminatory. This levels the playing field by making all American citizens equal under the eyes of the law. This does not eliminate discrimination. No law can be passed that will eliminate discrimination.

As you can tell from my writing, even I am prejudiced, against lawyers and socialists.

# Chapter 27
## *Amendment LI*

*During the term that a citizen is serving a sentence for any crime, to include probation, said citizen shall lose the right to vote in any election.*

Punishment for a crime should include the lost of citizenship for the duration of punishment. The person is a criminal because he does not want to honor our laws, be a valuable citizen, and support our society. Since they do not want to honor the law, they should have no say in the representative process until such time that society says they are cured.

The progressive, socialist crowd has been and is pushing to allow convicts to vote. This is just what we need in this country; criminals electing criminals.

# Chapter 28
## *Amendment LII*

*A citizen may own, buy, sell, or trade weapons without restriction or registration. For this purpose, weapon is defined as: handguns, rifles, shotguns, electronic weapons or devices, chemical dispensers, knives, and chemical loads. This is a citizen's right that shall not be infringed by law, tax, or other legal constraints.*

This country was founded upon the premise that Americans are self reliant and can take care of themselves.

For too long the government has told us that gun ownership is a safety hazard. This is an outright lie perpetuated by the government to disarm the citizens. Ten times more children accidentally die from bathtubs, bicycles, and skateboards than from gun accidents. If politicians were truly worried about child safety they would outlaw bathtubs, bicycles, and skateboards. Gun ownership is the most important right that a citizen might have. Fear of armed citizens is what keeps our government quasi honest.

Please notice that I said quasi honest. Nothing seems to keep politicians totally honest. They are like snakes. They slither in anywhere there is an opening.

# Chapter 29
## *Amendment LIII*

*A legal occupant of a house, building, business, or transportation vehicle may defend such area, self, or others, by the use of deadly force to thwart felonious activity, without the duty to retreat. Upon absolution, the legal occupant shall be held harmless from all legal action, criminal or civil.*

Citizens deserve the right to defend themselves, their loved ones, their property, and others' liberty in general, without fear of reprisal. When perpetuating a crime, a criminal should have no right to assume the victim will not be allowed by law to fight back.

# Chapter 30
## *Amendment LIV*

*Within four years after passage of this Amendment, a citizenship card shall be issued to and updated regularly at no charge to the citizen. The use of a false or altered citizenship card is punishable by a minimum of twenty years imprisonment. The citizenship card shall be presented at a polling station to vote.*

Most people do not want national identity cards. I, personally, do not want a national identity card. However our borders are so porous all citizens need to be identified. Until the borders are secured and all illegal aliens removed, we are hamstrung into actions we do not like. The identity card must be shown to an employer before hire. This would eliminate illegal aliens from holding jobs.

Since citizenship is the most important right in our life, we must protect it from theft by stringent punishment for violation of that right.

What I really wanted was to require that a person voting dip his right index finger in red indelible ink. It takes three days for the ink to wear off. The obvious advantage is that no person could vote twice in any election. However, a compromise had to be made to ensure that only citizens voted.

The argument was made that a national database could be setup. When a person voted, the card could be swiped. If the card had been swiped previously in any other polling place, the person would not be allowed to vote and could possibly be arrested on the spot.

Also the card should be free. That way no one can complain that it is a Jim Crow tax.

# Chapter 31
## *Amendment LV*

*The government shall not infringe into the personal lives of citizens beyond that which is necessary to enforce written laws.*

The lie detector is used to hire Government and contract employees. Courts have ruled lie detector results as unreliable, because the lie detector has a basic flaw. It can detect if a person has a conscience. People with a conscience will show an electronic reaction. People without a conscience will not have the same reaction. Consequently, the government is now staffed with people that have no concept of right and wrong, i.e., pathological liars. Without a conscience their idea of right and wrong is the same as that of an earthworm. If I like it, it is good. If I don't like it, it is bad. But to make matters worse, they have the "make believe" power of the Government behind them, which they exaggerate and aren't afraid to flaunt. Taking a lie detector test for employment purposes is an infringement upon the 5th Amendment right of non-self-incrimination. The concept of using a lie detector was started to protect the President from embarrassing situations. Nowhere in the Constitution does it say the Government must protect the President from embarrassing situations. Since it violates the Constitution and is not reliable, this practice must cease.

Also, how a citizen spends their hard earned cash is strictly up to the citizen. As long as the product or service is legal to purchase, the government should not be telling citizens, you shall buy this product or service. You shall buy a Chevrolet and not a Ford.

The Founding Fathers did not include personal safety in the Constitution. A person was expected to develop the intelligence to deal with everyday life. Personal safety was never and is not an issue where the government should be involved.

Under the Commerce Clause the government can control product and work place safety. Product safety covers such mundane things as child safety caps on medicine bottles and seat belts installed in vehicles. Work place safety covers such things as ear and eye protection while at work. However, when the government mandates, either directly or indirectly, individual safety rules, they are infringing upon a citizen's right.

There is a wide spread practice in the government to infringe upon citizen and state rights, but it is done indirectly such that it is not readily noticed.

Case in point: Years ago car manufacturers did not want to install airbags. The cost was too high. They ask the Department of Transportation (DOT) what could be done to eliminate that requirement. DOT responded that if it were law that people had to wear seat belts then airbags could be ignored. DOT wanted to pass a rule requiring people to wear seat belts. But, DOT reasoned that it could not pass such a rule because it had no way to enforce it. In an end around run, they told states that road construction monies would not be given to states that did not pass and enforce a seat belt law. En mass states passed seat belt laws. This saved the car companies millions of dollars. It was so sublime and insidious. This nefarious practice of coercion has been let loose upon an unsuspecting public.

This practice is not limited to DOT. States, counties, and cities have been directed to pass various laws or Federal grant money will not be disbursed.

# Chapter 32
## *Amendment LVI*

*Amendment XXVI to the Constitution of the United States is hereby rescinded. The minimum age of voting shall be at twenty one years of age. The minimum age of militia shall be at eighteen years of age.*

The argument was put forth years ago that if eighteen year olds could be drafted then they should be allowed to vote. Citizens though this made sense and allowed it to happen. But just the opposite occurred; eighteen year olds were too inexperienced with life and were too afraid to stand up for a just cause. They have been easily led by manipulative political groups and politicians into believing that cowardly appeasement and throwing money at a problem will make the problem go away. Since enactment of Amendment XXVI, this country has steadily gone downhill. Until these citizens learn the value of hard work and sacrifice and self esteem, they should not be allowed to vote.

Alcohol consumption is the domain of the states and shall remain as defined by the respective state

Those who do not study history are doomed to repeat it.

# Chapter 33
## *Amendment LVII*

*All Citizens are equally entitled to the free exercise of religion, according to their dictates of conscience. However, Judo-Christianity shall be the official religion of the Government of the United States of America and shall not be considered an infringement upon other religions, when exercised in the United States or territories. Any portion of a religion that violates the moral tenants of Judo-Christianity is an infringement on Judo-Christianity and shall not be entitled to nor enjoy protection under force of law.*

Our Founding Fathers assumed that only Europeans of the Judo-Christian persuasion would immigrate to America seeking religious freedom. Little did they realize that other religions would immigrant and then use our freedom of religion clause to attack the Judo-Christian faith. This is to correct that deficiency in the Constitution.

Animal sacrifice, polygamy, and slavery, among other things, would no longer be an acceptable religious practice allowed in this country.

A Christmas tree was a tradition even before the American Revolution. Even during the Revolution, soldiers took time to cut a pine tree and decorate it. Americans like to see a

Christmas tree and a nativity scene in the town square. It gave us a sense of belonging to a larger family. This is part of our shared culture, national heritage, and American tradition.

No place in the Constitution does it say that religion and government must be divorced. Thomas Jefferson was and is often misquoted to prove the founding father wanted separation of government and religion. What he said was that no Christian sect should control the Government. This Amendment would return us to the guiding principles established by the founding fathers and to our culture.

# Chapter 34
## *Amendment LVIII*

*Being the National religion, the Oath of Office by any elected or appointed official shall be sworn upon the Judo-Christian holy book and to the Judo-Christian Creator and shall not be construed as an infringement upon any other religion.*

Our politicians need to swear an honest oath. (I'm not saying they don't swear.) They need to understand that they will be judged by a much higher court; a Court over which they have no control.

# Chapter 35
## Amendment LIX

*Marriage is a Judo-Christianity term used to describe a legally binding contract between two willing participants of the opposite sex. It shall not be used on any official documentation to describe any other contractual arrangement.*

If two or more people of the same or opposite sex want to agree to a legally binding civil union contract, that is their business. To paraphrase Thomas Jefferson, "If a man wants to worship 50 Gods, it won't break my leg." However, I personally don't want my religious term, "Marriage", used to describe their living arrangements.

A civil union contract shall be respected in the same manner as a marriage, with all of the same advantages and hindrances. But, do not call it a marriage.

# Chapter 36
## *Amendment LX*

*Public monies shall not be used to fund abortions, except in cases of rape, incest, or risk to the mother's life.*

The first gift GOD gave man was free choice. Man was given the choice to eat the apple or not.

If man decides to commit murder that is his free choice. To write a law denying a person free choice is the Government taking away GODs gift to mankind. This is Satan saying the Government is smarter than GOD. Because of this, abortion does not violate the Judo-Christian teachings.

However to assuage the conscience of people who do not want to be part of this, public monies cannot be used for abortions, except as noted.

There will be those people that say the Government has laws on the book against murder, robbery, rape, etc. My argument is that these laws are after the fact laws. You commit a murder and are sent to jail. But conviction is after the crime has been committed.

Abortion laws are before the fact laws. Pro-Life people believe that abortion is murder. The law is to stop Doctors before they commit a murder.

From a purely secular point of view, the Government should not fund abortions. We need the younger generation to pay social security taxes to continue the present ponzi scheme.

# Chapter 37
## *Amendment LXI*

*Controlled substances shall not be legalized for general consumption or recreational use. Alcohol, tobacco, betel nut, and caffeine products are exempt from this Amendment.*

Controlled substances have mind altering properties that would prevent citizens from reaching their full potential and, thus, reduce their value as a citizen by interfering with the clear, rational thought required of a citizen.

# Chapter 38
## *Amendment LXII*

*Elected or appointed officials and their spouse shall neither be employed by nor receive monies or other compensation from a foreign entity during their term in office and for five years after the expiration of their term in office. Elected or appointed officials and their spouse shall neither be employed by nor receive monies or other compensation from a corporate entity during their term in office*

When an official or spouse receives foreign monies either during their term or within five years after, there are serious questions of loyalty to our country. This practice cannot be condoned. And violation of this Amendment should be considered as the high crime of treason.

When an official or spouse receives corporate monies during their term of office, there are serious questions of loyalty to our country. This practice can no longer be condoned.

We would expect an official to get a job after his term in office. However, to avoid the appearance of impropriety, foreign entities should not be involved in that job.

Spouse is included because "pillow talk" can be a big influence in the decision making process.

# Chapter 39
## *Amendment LXIII*

*All persons retired from government employment, such that they receive public monies, shall neither be employed by the Government as a private contractor nor shall they have controlling interest in a company employed by the Government. This restriction shall be for a period of five years after termination of Government employment.*

Higher up government employees retire and draw a retirement check from the government and immediately get a contractor job with the same government agency, either as a consultant or through a company they have controlling interest in. This is the worst form of double dipping. A time limit is imposed to reduce the influence to get the contract job. They can still work as a contractor for a company but they cannot have controlling interest in that company.

# Chapter 40
## *Amendment LXIV*

*The government shall be limited to a maximum of one embassy and one consulate in any one foreign country at any one time. Military bases are exempt from this article.*

The purpose of an embassy is to maintain dialog with a foreign power. The purpose of a consulate is to provide assistance to United States citizens. Anything more than one embassy and one consulate in any one country is a waste of U.S. taxpayer monies.

# Chapter 41
## *Amendment LXV*

*International Treaties and/or membership in International Organizations shall be subjugated to the Constitution.*

There is a push among our power hungry leaders to subjugate the Constitution to foreign treaties. This would allow other countries to tell United State citizens what they can and cannot do. This is a direct attack upon American sovereignty.

Our politicians wrongly assume that treaties made with foreign governments and organizations are equal to or greater than the Constitution. Since the Senate approves a treaty, it must be more important than that worthless piece of paper called The Constitution.

This is just a friendly reminder to the politicians of the order of things. Our Constitution is our document declaring our freedom and setting the law of the land (America). No other document, including treaties, can ever supersede the rights defined in the Constitution.

# Chapter 42
## *Amendment LXVI*

*Economic aid to foreign countries shall be limited to emergency disaster relief.*

Giving economic or military aid to foreign countries has proven to be a debacle. The majority of the money is stolen. As far as us buying their friendship, I would rather have an open enemy rather that a friend I bought and paid for. Bought friends have a tendency to turn on us the first chance they get.

But America, being a Christian nation, has a long standing tradition of helping people in times of need and this is the hallmark of Christian America. This Amendment will continue that tradition, but stop our government from trying to buy friendship.

# Chapter 43
## *Amendment LXVII*

*Persons illegally in the United States shall not be entitled to the same rights, privileges, or entitlements as a citizen, except to be treated humanely until deported.*

Back in the 1700s, any person living in America was considered a citizen. The Founding Fathers appear to have made a minor mistake in the Constitution by quite often referring to citizens as people. This has let the courts interpret that to mean any person in the United States is entitled to citizen rights. This would correct that mistake by eliminating illegal aliens from those rights. Courts would not have to provide a free lawyer; schools would not have to teach their children; hospitals would not have to treat them for free.

Jesus said we would always have the poor. In America that saying has been slightly skewed, we will always have illegal aliens among us. There is an underlying form of economic slave labor; unscrupulous people are taking advantage of illegal aliens through sub-par wages and/or no benefits. Who can the illegal aliens complain to? Economic slave labor is a long standing tradition used in the Mid-East but it has no place in our society.

Please note, *"until deported"*; this is interrupted to mean all legal jurisdictions should check citizenship of suspects and, unless held for a crime, shall forward people to be deported. There will be no releasing of illegal aliens back into American society. Any jurisdiction releasing illegal aliens back into American society should be punished as a violation of the law of the land.

# Chapter 44
## *Amendment LXVIII*

*The right of citizenship by birth shall not be bestowed to children born to a non-citizen.*

In the beginning America needed all the citizens it could get. That need is long gone and so the law should be changed accordingly. Illegal females come to this country to bear their progeny. Then they claim they must be allowed to stay here to raise the U.S. citizen. This does not advocate separating mother and child. This advocates sending both back to their place of origin.

# Chapter 45
## *Amendment LXIX*

*English shall be the only official language of the United States. All official documentation, proceedings, and communications shall be written or spoken in English. The Government shall not be held accountable to provide translation.*

Billions of dollars is wasted every year by the government translating documents. Legal immigrants should learn and use English. It should not be the Governments job to translate for illegal immigrants and other criminals. In years past immigrants were ecstatic to be allowed to come to the United States. They gladly tried to learn their new home language. Today, immigrants don't care. This is only a temporary stop to make money before going back to their real home. Why bother to learn a foreign language, (English)?

Language is the glue that holds a country together. At the founding of this country, an official language was not designated. The people were equally split between English and German. The Founding Fathers decided to wait and see which would dominate. By now, it is a clear which language has won.

# Chapter 46
## *Amendment LXX*

*At the end of each fiscal year, the Statement and Account of Receipts and Expenditures shall be totaled. Receipts shall never fall below expenditures for that respective year, with exception for periods of declared war and up to three years after hostilities have cease; a declining annual GDP; or in the event of a major natural disaster and one year after the disaster. Violation of this article shall be cause for each and all Representatives, Senators; President, Vice President, Cabinet Members; and Supreme Court Justices to be fined thirty percent of their annual salary for each year in violation during their tenure.*

Too many people think the government just prints money to spend. Our deficit continues to grow unchecked. Congress doesn't care. They buy votes with our tax money. By putting in automatic checks, hopefully, this will open eyes that we, the people, mean business. And not business as usual for politicians, which is to spend, spend, and spend.

Deficit spending is a hidden tax that someone, sooner or later, will have to pay. Either we pay it directly through taxes or we pay it indirectly through inflation. Sooner or later the repo man will be coming for his share.

(Since the Chinese own most of the American debt, that means you or your children might be working in the rice paddies to pay the debt.)

# Chapter 47
## *Amendment LXXI*

*All citizen and legal entities shall pay an equal share of the tax burden. Within four years of passage of this Amendment, no tax and no disbursement shall be graduated based upon income.*

*1. A flat rate tax on all income shall be instituted on all legal entities with no allowances or deductions.*

*2. The flat rate shall never exceed fifteen percent, except during a declared war or natural disaster and is limited to less than three years after war hostilities cease or one year after the natural disaster.*

A graduated tax scheme is discrimination. This Amendment will cause everyone to scream. Poor people and rich people, alike, should pay the same percentage of their income as tax.

Poor people will scream that they shouldn't have to pay taxes. If Congress wants to give it back, that is fine. But let them give it back after it is paid in. Only when poor people pay taxes will they realize that, just like everyone, you must have money coming in before you can have money going out.

This would level the playing field because every legal entity would pay the same fixed percentage with no deductions.

Corporations and rich people will scream they need deductions because they spend money to make money. Big money will scream because now all the deductions are gone.

Right now it is the middle class screaming. They don't make much, but they have to pay. They spend money buying gas and clothes to make money, but they don't get the deductions. They want the playing field to be level. They are tired of playing this football game where it is uphill to the goal post.

One good point for poor people, the poor people tax will be eliminated. I have had many people, even highly educated people, tell me that no such tax exists. But it does exist. In the 1930s when the Democrats set up social security they buried a poor people tax in it. Above a certain limit you pay no social security tax.

Here is how it works:
John makes $10,000, he pays 8.5% SS tax, which is $850.
Jim makes $100,000, he pays 8.5% SS tax on the first $100,000, which is $8500.
Ralph makes $1,000,000, he pays 8.5% SS tax on the first $100,000, which is $8500.
John and Jim paid 8.5% but Ralph only paid 0.85%.

You can see the tax is graduated for poor people to pay more. It is a poor people tax.

This levels out the playing field and will add more to social security. No more moaning and groaning about it going broke.

# Chapter 48
## *Amendment LXXII*

*Economic equality shall never be a mandate of the Government imposed upon the people. The United States Government shall not manipulate and regulate the economy, except during a declared war or natural disaster. This shall include artificial wage and price controls and the purchase of products or production capacity to control price.*

This is a capitalistic society. People vote on products with their wallet. Increasingly the government is turning this into a socialistic society and their main weapon is controlling price, either directly or indirectly. Directly, the government buys wheat and destroys it to keep the price of bread high. Indirectly, the government sets a minimum wage which drives prices up and makes everyone ask for higher pay. The net result is that the number of poor people always remains the same. The government must get out of thinking they can outsmart the marketplace. The Government must let the marketplace run free. This is the true meaning of capitalism. People and businesses must learn to sink or swim under their own power. No more should the Government help this guy get rich by making that guy poor.

My wife is beautiful. My neighbors' wives are not so beautiful. Does that mean I must share her with them because they want to bed a beautiful woman?

# Chapter 49
## *Amendment LXXIII*

*The United States Government shall not own, buy, or sell private enterprise, e.g. companies, corporations, or intangible assets thereof, e.g. stocks, bonds, except in the context of a retirement fund investment.*

The government now owns controlling shares in several corporations. These companies were considered too important to collapse. Our Founding Fathers did not envision the government owning any private business. Sink or swim on your own was their motto. If the government cannot run itself efficiently, why should we think they could run a private enterprise? People vote on products with their wallet. Let that vote be the vote that counts. That is what free enterprise is all about.

# Chapter 50
## *Amendment LXXIV*

*No citizen, except military personnel, shall be required to stand, bow, genuflect, salute, or otherwise show deference to any appointed or elected officials.*

It was once common to stand when a judge or the president entered a room to show respect. If an individual wants to stand, bow, genuflect, or otherwise show deference to an appointed or elected official that is allowable. But citizens that do not want to show respect can no longer be forced to do so.

The only exception to this is military personnel. Standing and saluting in the military is not to show respect for the person. It is to show deference to the military rank.

Since all elected and appointed official are equal in rank to us, we should not be required to show deference due to rank.

# Chapter 51
## *Amendment LXXV*

*Retirement pay for all government employees, to include the President, is hereby capped at the mean average citizen's income. Retirement pay may increase or decrease each calendar year. This Amendment shall take effect three years after passage. A written guarantee of retirement pay prior to this Amendment shall not be honored.*

The government has repeatedly said that social security is to be limited to subsistence level. If the average citizen is limited to subsistence level then government employees should likewise be so limited. Retirement pay generated prior to this Amendment is included in this cap. Government retirees should not be living high on the hog while the rest of us are in the mud.

This is a wake up call to the Government that the entire retirement system needs an overhaul. The original concept was that Government employees would be paid less than their civilian counterparts. In exchange for that, they would get a more generous retirement allowance. Now they get higher pay than their civilian counterpart and in most cases their retirement pay is higher than a civilian counterpart that is still working.

The whole remuneration system is out of whack and must be revised.

To quell lawsuits, this is not an Ex Post Facto law. Retirement pay is a gift by the Government to employees for a job well done. The amount of the gift may be raised or lowered at any time as dictated by law.

# Chapter 52
## *Amendment LXXVI*

*Amendment XXVII is hereby rescinded. Each fiscal year, the Secretary of the Treasury shall calculate and publish the mean average citizen's income. All Citizens over eighteen years of age shall be included in the calculation of the average. Three years after ratification of this Amendment the revised wages and benefits for Government officials shall take effect.*

*The President, Vice President, and Supreme Court Justice compensation shall increase or decrease each calendar year and shall not exceed five times the mean average citizen's income and shall include no special benefits beyond that of the median wage earning citizen.*

*Congressional compensation shall increase or decrease each calendar year and shall not exceed four times the mean average citizen's income and shall include no special benefits beyond that of the median wage earning citizen.*

This Amendment will remove Congress from setting their own compensation by establishing their pay scale against the citizen's income, thus putting it beyond their control. The only special benefit of being an official is being paid above average wages. Once removed from office they should not receive any special benefits that a normal citizen does not have.

This also removes restrictions on raising or lowering wages of the officials.

Yearly readjustment means that in economic hard times the Federal outlay of funds will be reduced.

# Chapter 53
## *Amendment LXXVII*

*A Citizen Oversight Branch of the Government shall be established that is equal in power and not subservient to the Executive, Judicial, and Legislative Branches.*

*The Oversight Branch shall not be elected and shall have oversight authority advocated in this Amendment.*

*Initially, there shall be one Oversight Panel for:*
*1. Environment Control*
*2. Officials*
*3. Land Management*
*4. Compensation*

*Majority decisions of the Panel are legally binding. Decisions may be reversed only by an act of Congress.*

*Each Panel shall consist of five people.*

*One will be appointed by the Judicial Branch of the Government.*

*One will be appointed by the House of Representatives.*

*These two members shall be approved by the Senate.*

*The three additional members shall be conscripted in a random drawing from all voting age Citizens, excluding sitting or ex-sitting elected or appointed officials.*

*At any given time a panel shall not contain more than two members that are authorized to practice law.*

*At any given time a panel shall not contain two or more members from any one state.*

*A person may only serve in the Oversight Branch once in their lifetime for a period not to exceed five years.*

*Compensation shall be at the same rate as a member of the House of Representatives.*

*Each year, one or more member of each panel shall be replaced. The initial assembled panel shall draw lots to determine the initial length of service.*

*All panels shall convene three years after passage of this Amendment.*

*Members of a panel are restricted to their original panel where assigned.*

*New Panels may be incorporate after adoption of a defined charter approved by a majority vote of all panel's members and Congress.*

*A Panel member may be purged by an eighty percent vote of that panel.*

*A Panel may be dissolved upon an eighty percent vote of that panel.*

*A Panel decision requires a sixty percent vote of that panel.*

*The House of Representative may censor any Panel that strays outside the boundary of their charter. The Supreme Court may censor any Panel for a second occurrence. The President may censor any Panel for a third occurrence. Three different documented occurrences in the order specified are cause for dissolution and reestablishment of that Panel with new members.*

The main point of this Amendment is to empower the fourth branch of the United States government. The fourth branch has always been assumed to be the people. But as recent events have shown, the voice of the people is not that important to politicians. Therefore, the fourth branch must be established, recognized, and given power under the Constitution. But as has been proven again and again, people in power can be corrupted. The churning process must be fast to reduce complacency. The majority of the Oversight Branch must be common ordinary citizens. And the only way that can happen is through conscription. But even with all the controls, a Panel may run out of control. A three strike safeguard was put in place that requires input from all branches of the Government. No one branch of the Government should have complete control over the Oversight Branch. I'm afraid it is not perfect but it is the best that can be devised.

# Chapter 54
## *Amendment LXXVIII*

*A Citizens Oversight Panel shall have authority to bring charges of impeachment against elected or appointed officials, to include Judges, Senators, and Cabinet Members for violation of this Constitution, breach of national security, dereliction of duty, or other high crimes.*

The Founding Fathers did not put a clear clause in the Constitution to control wayward Judges, Senators, and Cabinet Members. It was assumed that judges were appointed for life because they were honest; senator would be controlled by their respective state; and the president would control his cabinet. This is not working properly. A clearly defined oversight panel must be established for the good of the country.

# Chapter 55
## *Amendment LXXIX*

*Unless a clear, critical, and undeniable contribution to the ecosystem is defined, no environmental controls may be enforced, such that it affects the main economic welfare of any Citizen. A Citizens Oversight Panel shall have authority to dismiss, approve, or compromise the suggested environmental controls.*

How many times have we heard where an entire community has lost its livelihood because of some supposedly endangered species? A little fish or worm is more important to the government than taking care of human life. I'm not saying that the little fish or worm is not important. Each case must be carefully thought about and the human circumstance must be considered in the equation. All Government agencies, including the EPA has a charter they must follow. This charter does not allow for the human factor. The goal of the Oversight Panel is to put human life back into the equation concerning environmental issues.

# Chapter 56
## *Amendment LXXX*

*A Citizens Oversight Panel shall review wages, salary, retirement pay, expenses, and benefits for elected and appointed officials and shall have authority to deny or affirm the rate and type.*

Hopefully the oversight panel will keep the Treasury Department honest.

# Chapter 57
## *Amendment LXXXI*

*A Citizens Oversight Panel shall review land acquisition and land and resource disposition and shall have authority to order disposition of excess lands or resources. Monies from the disposed properties shall only be used to pay against the national debt.*

What is wrong with this scenario? We have conserved enough natural resources to pay off the national debt. But the government wants to save it for future generations.

At the rate we are going the only people to enjoy this conservation will be the Chinese when they come to collect their debt. I would rather pay off the debt and worry about conservation when we can afford it.

Right now our main concern is to reduce the national debt. Sell the vehicle that is sitting on blocks in the front yard. What good is that vehicle if the repo man takes the house?

The politicians keep telling us that conserving all that land and resources is a savings account for future generations. The foreclosure notice is coming. It is time to take money out of that savings account and pay the debt.

# Chapter 58
## *Amendment LXXXII*

*Daylight Savings time shall cease to exist.*

Common people do not see a savings with daylight saving time and it is actually detrimental to their well being. But Congressmen want that extra hour to play golf in the summer. Let's keep the same time all year. The fewer disruptions that occur in our life the better it is for all of us.

If the Congressmen want to play golf, let them reset their alarm clock. Don't make all the people do it.

# Chapter 59
## *Amendment LXXXIII*

*The government shall no longer recognize unions or other organizations that represent government employees.*

The Government should not be held hostage by any organization.

Unions at one time were very necessary. The Government only listened to the socialist big businesses that wanted cheap slave labor. The unions forced the Government to pass laws. Because of this, unions in the private sector have outlived their usefulness.

For the union bosses to make money, the Government is now the target. Unions in the Government sector are growing because the people approving union contract are usually union members or former union members. Unions are the biggest stumbling block to the government functioning more efficiently. The workings of the government will not be harmed by the lack of unions. There will be no more, "I can't do that, union rules says I can't."

On a personal note, thousands of West Virginia rednecks died in the Mine Wars. They wore a red handkerchief around their neck to differentiate between combatants and non-combatants. The US Army battle cry was, "Kill the rednecks." The name now means any person dumb enough to fight the Government. In the end, West Virginia miners won the war. No more eight years olds had to work in the mines. Mine safety laws were passed. Lunch hour was authorized for workers. Bet you didn't know that. Thousands of West Virginia rednecks died just so you could have a lunch break.

Be a redneck and support making America great.

# Chapter 60
## *Amendment LXXXIV*

*If a budget cannot be approved by the end of the fiscal year, then the previous year budget shall take effect and may not be revised until the following year. Emergency spending, except for a declared war or natural disaster, shall not be allowed.*

No real budget has been approved in three years but the Government keeps on spending money. No budget should mean no money will be spent. Article 1, Section 9 of the Constitution says, no money can be drawn from the treasury unless appropriated during the budget and reconciling process.

But the politician have such little regard for WE, the people, they keep on spending. They have total disregard for the Constitution. Here is how they do it. Congress has divided up the budget into little emergency pieces of pork. The definition of emergency is; we are running out of money to spend. This emergency is approved for sixty days, that one for ninety days, etc. Then the next time it is thirty days for this one and one hundred twenty days for that one. After three years of this the budget is in such a shambles no one knows for sure how much, where, or when. This has got to be the biggest joke ever played on the American people.

Everything dealing with the budget is now considered an emergency.

We want a clearly defined budget. We want only real emergencies to be called emergencies.

We want the budget to be balanced. No more deficit spending.

# Chapter 61
## *Amendment LXXXV*

*Government free franking privileges are hereby abolished.*

The Constitution states that the Post Office is equal in importance to the Department of Defense. Congress treats the Post Office as if were a bastard stepchild. The Post Office must be raised in stature. The Post Office delivers Government mail for free.

The Department of Defense doesn't send a soldier to assist every police officer in stopping people for speeding. The Department of State doesn't send an official with every tourist to a foreign country. Why should the Post Office be required to give out free service? We the citizens are paying for this by increased rates of our postage. This is a hidden tax on all citizens that use the Post Office. Put it in the budget where we can see it. Let franking be included in each department's budget.

Congress wants to dissolve the Post Office because it is working in the red. A lot of this red ink comes from the actions of Congress. Make the Government pay postage like every other good citizen.

And if Congress is worried about the Post Office making money, stop giving corporation big cuts in postage rates. Let them pay their fair share. I am sick of all the junk mail I receive. You give all other agencies free reign to do whatever they want to do. Quit micromanaging the Post Office.

# Chapter 62
## *Amendment LXXXVI*

*Elected or appointed officials shall not enjoy the right of non self incrimination.*

When officials are elected or appointed, they should be aware that certain individual citizen rights are no longer in effect. They are no longer citizens; they are public servants. Too many elected and appointed officials are using the 5th Amendment to cover their own deficiencies and dishonesties. Being an elected or appointed official is a public trust and, as such, requires openness to public scrutiny. For an elected or appointed official to deny information to the public is to violate that public trust by declaring oneself as more important than the Government and people that they serve.

The idea that the people must serve the official is ludicrous. The Government was founded on the principle; of the people, by the people, and for the people. Nowhere in the Declaration of Independence or the Constitution does it say that the people must serve a Government official's private goal or hidden agenda.

The politician's objective should be the general welfare of the people and not their personal gain.

# Chapter 63
## *Amendment LXXXVII*

*All Primary Elections shall be held on the second Tuesday of May. Candidates need only pay a minimal recording fee to be placed on the ballot.*

A lot of people think that the primary election is to determine the political party nominee for the general election. Nothing can be farther from the truth. The political party can change a nominee, even after the primary.

The argument has been made that the primary election is discriminatory. A few states control the entire process. Win a few states at the beginning of primary season and that person is then pushed all the way to become the candidate. The states at the end of the primary season have no real choice of nominee.

The Government has the right to declare when the primary election shall be held and the responsibility to remove all discrimination factors from the ballot. Having all Federal primary elections on the same day levels the playing field for all potential candidates and all voting citizens.

# Chapter 64
## *A Second Dream*

In 2009, I had another dream that came from GOD. This was to tell me what would happen if America did not repent.

I was in the hills. A dirt road, which was wide enough for six vehicles, was in front of a two story stone house, which had stairs with three steps up to a porch along the entire front of the house. Separating the road from the yard was a rough stone wall, about three foot high. The only opening in the wall was a white picket gate on the sidewalk that ran to the stairs. I couldn't see around the house. But, I knew that the wall went all the way around the property.

The house was an orphanage, with an old woman in charge. The children were playing in the yard. A monster, very similar to what people would think of as a werewolf was leaning against a porch pillar on one foot. His legs are crossed, as were his arms across his broad chest. The monster is not asleep. His eyes are open; he watches the children as they play.

A large caravan of shiny black limousines approach, stop, and people get out. The leader gets out of his expensive car and approaches the gate. The old woman comes running out to meet him. He says he has come for the children to give them a better life as slaves for his minions, wives, and concubines.

The old woman says, "Please leave, I am trying to save you."

He can't open the gate. Some unearthly power stops him. His minions say, "See, we told you. She did the same thing to us." The monster on the porch uncrosses his feet and stands on two feet, like a human, but still leaning against the porch pillar.

The leader says, "I don't care. Take the children."

Dozens of minions pull out guns and aim at the old woman. The old woman says, "Stop, I am trying to save you." And, they begin to fire, riddling the old woman with bullets. The children run into the house. Even as she is falling, the old woman says, "Stop, I am trying to save you." The monster continues to lean against the porch pillar. The firing stops.

Although lying on the ground, with a multitude of gunshots, the old woman says, "Stop, I am only trying to save you."

The leader gives a hand gesture to one of his minions, who fires one more time, killing the woman. The monster leaps from the porch, across the yard, and over the wall. The minions fire wildly with several of the bullets striking the monster. The bullets have no effect. The monster runs off down the road behind the limousines. The leader turns to look at the house.

From behind him comes screams of terror as the monster starts at the last car ripping the occupants and car to pieces. The leader continues to look at the house and tells his closest minions to take care of that and flippantly point his thumb backwards. The leader continues to look at the house, thinking of his coming fun of debasing, torturing, and killing the helpless children.

Howls, screams, and gunshots fill the air behind the leader. Then everything becomes quiet. The leader lost in his revelry of the coming pleasures slowly realizes that the sounds have stopped. He turns to thank his minions. And there stands the monster. A fleeting look of terror passes over his face and he runs. The monster gives chase. Around the country they run, to and fro. The leader is constantly cajoling more minions to take up his fight and kill the monster.

But the monster keeps coming and the minions continue to fall to the monster. Finally when there are no more minions, the leader turns to fight. A mighty battle it is; but the monster prevails.

The monster calmly goes back to the orphanage, climbs the steps, and leans against a porch pillar on one foot, crossing his feet and arms. The children come out to play. The old woman comes out of the house to watch over the children.

This prophecy deals only with America. It is not a worldwide prophecy and should not be included with or used to try to explain the Book of Revelations.

The interpretation I was given is simple. The old woman is our belief in GOD and liberty. The monster is the people of America. The children are just that, the children of America. The opposition is the mass of unbelievers that control our Government.

The meaning is elementary. If we don't do something now, then, at some time in the future, we will have to water the Tree of Liberty with blood. The choice is yours.

# Chapter 65
## *Conclusion*

I found this article circulating on the internet. I would gladly give the author credit, but the author is unknown. It is far more eloquent than anything I could write. It says on one page what I have been trying to express in previous seventy pages.

In his proclamation of 1863 for a nationwide day of fasting and prayer, Abraham Lincoln, this great president said: "It is the duty of nations, as well as of men, to owe their dependence upon the over-ruling power of GOD...and to recognize that those nations only are blessed whose GOD is the LORD:...We have grown in numbers, wealth and power as no other nation has grown; but we have forgotten GOD! We have forgotten the gracious HAND which preserved us in peace, and multiplied and enriched and strengthened us; and we have vainly imagined in the deceitfulness of our hearts, that all these blessings were produced by some superior wisdom and virtue of our own."

And because Lincoln saw a nation that had forgotten GOD; a nation drunk with success not due to its own efforts; a nation taking all the credit to itself, this great president called upon the nation for a day of fasting and prayer to confess this national sin before GOD. The fate of the nation hung in the balance when he issued that proclamation. But GOD heard and answered that great national prayer offering, and the nation was preserved! Abraham Lincoln knew these great material blessings had not been earned, but had been given to our people by the GOD of Abraham, Isaac, and Jacob.

GOD help our leaders to see this thing as Abraham Lincoln saw it, to call upon the nation as President Lincoln called upon this nation for the deadly-earnest, heart-rending fasting and prayer, to issue a proclamation as President Lincoln did setting apart a definite day for this confession of sin before GOD, for repentance, calling upon GOD to intervene and help and save us by putting our trust in HIM.

Since September 11, 2001, the United States and its brethren in the British nations have mourned the deadly results of a heinous terrorist attack on the United States. But, while the nations have mourned, they have not begun the process of turning from their sins. The sins that caused the loss of protection from their GOD who has heaped abundant blessings upon them; and because they have not openly turned from their rebellion against GOD's laws, it is obvious the future holds even more severe punishments for the nations.